THE
TREE PLANTER'S
SURVIVAL GUIDE

(Almost) Everything You Need to Know to Become a Tree Planter and Survive Your First Season

THE TREE PLANTER'S SURVIVAL GUIDE

(Almost) Everything You Need to Know to Become a Tree Planter and Survive Your First Season

KEVIN MILLER

Copyright © 2019 Kevin Miller

All rights reserved. No part of this publication may be reproduced, distributed, or transmitted in any form or by any means without prior written permission from the author, except brief excerpts for review purposes.

ISBN: 9781095685372

Cover illustrations by Larry Metz

Kevin Miller
Box 380
Kimberley, BC, Canada V1A 2Y9

www.kevinmillerxi.com

CONTENTS

INTRODUCTION   7

1 – WHAT IS TREE PLANTING?   9
   Who Pays for It All?   10
   A Day in the Life   10
   Where Does Tree Planting Take Place?   13
   When Does Tree Planting Happen?   14

2 – HOW MUCH MONEY DO TREE PLANTERS MAKE?   15
   The Secret Ingredient to a Successful Season   16
   Calibrate Your Expectations   18

3 – HOW TO GET A JOB AS A TREE PLANTER   21
   When Should You Apply?   23
   Special Information for Foreign Workers   23
   Directory of Tree Planting Companies   24

4 – WHAT IT COSTS TO TREE PLANT AND WHAT YOU'LL NEED TO DO IT   33
   Transportation   33
   Tree Planting Gear   34
   Personal Gear   38
   The Bottom Line   45
   Where to Buy Your Gear   45

5 – HEALTH AND SAFETY   47
   General Tips   47

Physical Preparation for Tree Planting	49
A Word About Wildlife	50
CONCLUSION	**53**
GLOSSARY OF TREE PLANTING TERMS	**55**
OTHER TREE PLANTING RESOURCES	**59**
TREE PLANTING LOG BOOK	**61**
ABOUT THE AUTHOR	**63**
ENJOYED THIS BOOK?	**64**

INTRODUCTION

Every year, a whopping 3.5–7 billion trees are harvested from Canada's forests, with the bounty used for everything from construction materials to chopsticks to toilet paper. Each summer, approximately 500 million of those trees are replaced by hand by a mighty band of misfits known as tree planters. These hardy individuals spend a few months enduring some of the harshest working conditions imaginable in pursuit of adventure, excitement, carbon offsets, and cold hard cash. Bugs, bears, blisters, hailstorms, freezing nights, bad food, diarrhea, grumpy foremen, repetitive-stress injuries, intense short-term romances, and loneliness are just some of the hazards you will face as a tree planter. In fact, tree planting was featured on the TV show *World's Toughest Jobs*, and the three guys who tried it didn't even last a week!

For most of those who manage to survive the season, the rewards far outweigh the toll that tree planting takes on their mind, body, and spirit. In addition to earning a good living—veteran planters can make $15,000 or more in a two-month season—tree planting is a great way to meet all sorts of interesting people from across the country and around the world. It also allows you to access remote wilderness areas that most people never get to see. And like running a triathlon, surviving a season of tree planting gives you bragging rights, putting you in an elite class of men and women who have pushed themselves to the limit and survived to tell the tale—which they are prone to do at parties with only a minimal amount of alcohol and prompting.

If you think you have what it takes to join this privileged few, but you don't know where to begin, then this book is for you. Not only will it show you how to get a job as a tree planter, it will explain how to make the most of your season and how to endure the heat, cold, rain, mud, black flies, mosquitoes, cuts, scrapes, chafing, back strain, and beaver fever, and possibly make you rich in the process—or at least wealthy enough to give you a jump start on that student loan or your savings account for that backpacking trip to Europe you've always dreamed about.

1

WHAT IS TREE PLANTING?

Let's begin with the basics. Tree planting is the manual method of replacing trees in an area that has been logged or devastated by a forest fire. And when I say *manual*, I mean exactly that: by hand. When it comes to tree planting, labor-saving devices are few and far between. Therefore, planters need to be in good physical condition. And if you're not in good physical condition at the start of the season, you'll look and feel like a champion by the end! Consider it the best weight-loss/cardio program going—and you get paid to do it!

In terms of gear, each planter is equipped with a specialized shovel—usually a D-handle spade with a long narrow blade—and a set of bags that hang from the waist with straps that also go over the shoulders, similar to a backpack. Into these bags, planters stuff bundles of seedlings, calculating how many they will need to get across their planting area and back, so they don't have to waste time running back to the cache to reload. (Count on wearing twenty to thirty pounds of trees around your waist all day.) The foreman's job is to race around on a quad ensuring each planter is continually stocked with trees, so they don't get stuck waiting for a new box to be delivered.

Planters don't actually dig holes for the trees. Rather, they look for a suitable place to plant a tree, as dictated by the contract. Usually this is a high spot with exposed soil or only a thin layer of humus (a.k.a. "duff" covering the soil. Once the planter has found a spot, he or she clears the area of debris (or adds debris, in the rare cases where the contract requires it), jams his or her shovel into the ground, kicks it once or twice, and then wedges the soil open until there's enough space in which to slide the seedling down the back of the shovel and into the dirt. Once the tree is in the ground, the planter slides the shovel out of the ground, kicks the hole shut, tugs on the tree to ensure it's snug, and then moves on to plant the next tree. This process can take anywhere from a few seconds to a minute depending on the type of ground and the planter's skill and experience level. Once you learn the basics of planting, refining your technique is a never-ending quest in your search for speed.

Who Pays for It All?

The responsibility for reforestation rests with the forestry companies that own the rights to harvest the trees from a given area. Rather than do the work themselves, these companies subcontract the job to tree planting companies which, in turn, hire people like you to pick up a shovel, strap on some planting bags, and slam the seedlings into the ground.

Due to the makeup of Canada's boreal forests, the most common types of trees planted are pine, spruce, and fir. The type of trees planted in an area vary according to the type of ground, the types of trees that were growing there before, and the types of trees the forestry companies would like to harvest in the future. Each contract dictates the types of trees to be planted and how many. It takes about thirty years until the trees you plant are ready for harvest, so if you're still around by then, you can go back up north and see things come full circle.

A Day in the Life

A typical day in the life of a tree planter consists of waking up *early* in the morning (5:30 a.m. is not unusual), having a quick breakfast, and then going off to work for anywhere from eight to twelve hours.

Because it's not always possible to stay where the planting takes place, tree planters often have to drive to work, just like everyone else. The drive may be anywhere from five minutes to an hour over rough logging roads. Some companies supply comfortable modern vehicles. If you're really lucky, you may even be flown in by helicopter! Other companies put planters on an old school bus. I hated riding the bus as a kid, never mind as a tree planter. In my first year, our crew went through three school buses in a single season—one of which lost a wheel as we were riding in it. I'm not sure if we spent more time pushing those buses or riding in them. In other cases, a vehicle is a luxury, and you may have to walk for up to thirty minutes from your campsite to the block (the place where the trees are planted).

Once you arrive on the block, prepare to spend the entire day walking for miles across rocky, uneven terrain covered by tree stumps, logs, bogs, slash piles, and other hazards as you struggle to find a place to plant anywhere from 1,000 to 4,000 seedlings. That's right, folks, 1,000 to 4,000 seedlings *per day*.

Due to the marathon nature of the job, tree planting does not require a lot of brute strength, although strength can be an asset. Endurance is the key. If you are questioning whether or not you can do the job, try not to think about doing it all at once, or it will seem overwhelming. Don't ask yourself if you can handle two months of tree planting; ask yourself if you can handle a single day. Anyone can plant a single tree. The hard part is doing it over and over again, thousands of times per day. The repetitive work, compounded by loneliness, boredom, bugs, and bad weather, is a big reason why many people say that being successful at tree planting is more of a mental game than a physical one.

The majority of planters are college students and poor, misguided foreigners who were led to believe that tree planting was a great way to make money and see the country, but some people plant well into their forties. While most tree planters are males, more and more women are grabbing a shovel and trying it out. Some foreman are leery of hiring women, because they assume they won't last the season or won't plant as many trees as a guy. However, some of the best planters I know are women. So, ladies, don't be afraid to give it a go. There's no better opportunity to demolish a stereotype and show up the buff guy with gym muscles who thinks he's God's answer to climate change.

There are no prescribed coffee or lunch breaks during planting. Speaking from experience, take as little time as possible for breaks, because they tend to kill momentum. And remember, if you're not planting, you're not earning money, so slam down that sandwich, and get back out there!

In addition, tree planting is highly competitive. Not only is everyone competing to plant the highest number of trees each day (it's an ego thing), they're also competing for the best ground—that is, the ground with the fewest obstacles. The fastest planters—and, if I'm honest, those who do the best job of sucking up to the boss—tend to get the best ground. If you're a "new kid on the block," so to speak, a rookie, prepare to plant some nasty ground until you prove yourself worthy of something better. The only way to do that is to post some good numbers without sacrificing quality for speed.

The sooner you finish your section, the sooner you go on to the next section. The same goes for your planting contract as a whole. The sooner it's complete, the sooner you can move on to the next one. Due to the limited number of days available for planting, companies want to get as many trees in the ground as possible within the shortest amount of time. For this reason, many companies work six out of every seven days. (The number of days worked and the length of time work each day tends to increase as you get closer to the end of a contract.) Some companies do a three-or-four-days-on, one-day-off rotation, which they believe allows for better recovery time and helps keep their planters highly motivated and less prone to injury. I tend to agree with this philosophy.

Once quitting time comes, the planters pile back into the vehicles and rumble back to camp. Supper is usually ready when everyone arrives, and in most cases, the cooks and the food are excellent. With tree planters burning anywhere between 5,000–7,000 calories per day, food becomes an all-consuming passion. Knowing this, most companies make sure not to skimp in this regard. That said, during my first year, we were only allowed one slice of processed meat in our sandwiches for lunch. The rest of our sandwiches had to be peanut butter and jam, which came out of white five-gallon buckets. That and we had French toast *every* morning. I think the only reason why the cook stayed on for the season was she was sleeping with one of the foreman. At any rate, it's a wonder I still like peanut butter today, although I still can only barely tolerate French toast. If you find yourself on such a crew, start casting around for another one. There's no reason for you to put up with such treatment. I'm still not sure why we didn't mutiny.

On the ride home or while eating supper, planters report their tallies for the day—i.e., how many trees they've planted. To keep track of this, planters peel the stickers off each box of seedlings they plant. Word to the wise: don't lose your stickers! Without them, if your numbers don't match the numbers of your foreman or supervisor, their numbers will determine what you get paid. This is where the competitiveness and egos really come out, not to mention the insults—all in good fun, of course. (Yeah, right!)

After a quick shower and perhaps a visit around the campfire, everyone goes off to their tent (or, if they're lucky, motel room) for the night. Unless there's a really good reason to stay up late, tree planters usually hit the sack early. As the saying goes, "Morning comes early!" Some planters find it necessary to blow off steam by doing such things as smoking pot or drinking excessively in the evenings. My advice is to save such activities for your days off—better yet, wait until the end of the season. Try a good book, a TV show or a movie you downloaded from Netflix (you did download movies and TV shows the last time you were in town, right?) or some music instead. You will feel much better in the morning, and you'll make a lot more money.

In addition to planting trees, planters are often called upon to do "volunteer" work, such as helping set up camp and loading and unloading boxes of trees when they're delivered to the site, and everyone is expected to pull their weight. So, before you start grumbling when you're asked to help unload a reefer (refrigerator) truck that got into camp at 11:30 p.m. just as you were falling asleep, remember that without trees, you can't plant tomorrow. Besides, do you really want everyone to hate you in the morning, because you were the only one who wouldn't get out of bed? Some companies pay for this type of labor in addition to what you make planting. That is something you should check into when applying for a job.

Where Does Tree Planting Take Place?

Tree planting takes place across Canada, primarily in the northern regions of each province. As indicated earlier, some planting also takes place in southwestern Ontario and southern BC. Exactly where planting takes place varies from year to year and even from contract to contract. You may find yourself planting quite close to a city or town on one contract—and if you're really score, staying in a motel!—and then have to move four or five hours into the bush, where the only vestiges of civilization are a couple of logging camps you pass along the way. Trust me, if you're stuck in a leaky tent all summer, you'll never view an ATCO trailer with such longing!

Planting in BC is centered around towns and cities like Prince George, Smithers, Kamloops, Cranbrook, Kelowna, and Revelstoke. In Alberta, tree planting tends to take place north of Edmonton, around communities like Grand Prairie. In Saskatchewan, tree planters can be found roaming around places like Meadow Lake and Prince Albert on their days off. If you've ever wanted to see the land of lakes and trees north of Winnipeg, Manitoba is the place for you. Shania Twain fans who plant in Ontario will likely get a chance to check out her hometown of Timmins while also planting around places like Hearst and Thunder Bay. Planting also takes place in the northern regions of Quebec, around the communities of Abitibi, Mauricie, and the Gaspé Peninsula, and in various parts of the Maritimes. So, despite what I said earlier about misguided foreigners, tree planting truly is a great way to experience practically every region of the country, seeing remote parts of Canada in their pristine glory.

When Does Tree Planting Happen?

The bulk of tree planting takes place in May and June each year, although some shorter contracts take place earlier in the year and throughout the summer. It all depends on the location. For example, in the southern coastal regions of British Columbia and on Vancouver Island, planting can begin as early as February or March. Tree planters typically sign on to a two-month contract for the spring season. If they're really die hard or desperate for cash and glory, they pick up one or two shorter contracts for the summer. But these contracts usually go to veteran planters only. Job doing other forestry-related work, such as brush-cutting and pruning, are also available for the summer. Ask around once you're up there.

2

HOW MUCH MONEY DO TREE PLANTERS MAKE?

Now that you have a good overview of the job, let's get down to what really matters: money. Tree planters are paid by the tree, with current prices ranging from 8.5 to 25 cents per tree. Generally speaking, the harder it is to plant the trees, the higher the price per tree will be.

Factors that affect the price per tree include the condition of the ground—whether or not it's rocky, covered with debris, or steep—and the types of trees being planted. For example, some trees have bare roots, which look like a ten-year-old kid with bedhead. These roots have to be corralled together and then swept into the hole, pointing straight down. This really slows down the planting process, because you have to dig a deeper hole and ensure the roots are straight rather than J-shaped, requiring a higher price per tree. Other trees come in sleek cones that are easy to slip into the soil. Areas that have been burned are usually easier to plant than areas that have been logged. But sometimes even burnt ground can be tough. If might look like a sandy beach, but beneath that brown layer of ash could be several inches of duff that you have to dig through before you can plant a tree.

Sometimes the ground is scarified, or the debris left over from the logging process is plowed into hedgerows, making planting much easier. In fact, on one contract I planted, the ground was furrowed, just like a farmer's field. On that contract, I averaged around 3,500 trees per day. The most difficult ground to plant is rocky soil and steep hillsides, because they take a toll on the body, your shovel constantly dinging off rocks as you probe for dirt, and make it much harder to find a suitable location to plant a tree.

The Secret Ingredient to a Successful Season

The price per tree is only one factor that determines how much a tree planter makes. The other major factor is self-discipline. No one can make you any money out there on the block except you. Therefore, how much you get out of tree planting is dependent largely on what you put into it.

Even in the best conditions—like the furrows I just mentioned, which I encountered in my third season—the most I've ever been able to plant in a single day is 3,500 trees. I believe we were getting seven cents per tree on that job. That comes out to $245/day. It's much more typical to plant somewhere between 1,000–2,000 trees per day. So, at 8 cents per tree, that's somewhere between $80–$160. That doesn't sound like much, because it isn't! But at 8 cents per tree, unless you're just starting out, you're definitely going to be at or exceeding 2,000 trees per day. Once you've been at it a while and know what you're doing, count on making over $200 per day on most contracts during your first year. Stretch that over an eight-week season, and you're looking at around $9,600, assuming you work for 6 days a week and make at least $200 per day. That's a nice chunk of change, but don't forget to deduct camp costs (about $25/day), equipment costs (it could cost you anywhere from $500–$1,500 to gear up for the season), and transportation costs to and from wherever you're planting (more on this in a later chapter). Even so, if you work hard, you can still walk away with a nice wad of cash by the end of the season. Veterans can regularly make $500 or more per day. Most planters report earning the equivalent of $25–$27 per hour.

Keep this in mind though: when it comes to tree planting, there are no guarantees. The weather may crap out. You may wind up with horrible land for the entire season, because your foreman ticked off his boss, or you may suffer an injury that slows you down or tanks your season. One year I planted with some guys from Newfoundland who flew all the way out to BC hoping to make huge, steaming piles of cash. It turned out they weren't prepared for the hard work, and most of them struggled to earn enough money just to get back home. The good news is, these days, tree planting companies will top up each planter's earnings to at least minimum wage during each pay period, including overtime, where applicable. Ask your company if they adhere to this practice.

Unlike other jobs, in many cases, tree planters do not receive a paycheck once per week or even biweekly, although some of the larger companies offer a direct deposit every two weeks. What usually happens is first the land is planted. Then the company that contracted the land to be planted checks the trees to ensure they are up to standard. Finally, a decision is made as to whether the tree planting company will receive the full price of the contract, whether some or all areas need to be replanted, or whether a penalty will be handed out for poor quality. The penalty usually comes in the form of a partial payment. In other words, instead of getting ten cents per tree, you only get eight cents. Other penalties, in the form of fines, can also be handed out to a company, a crew, or an individual planter. Some examples of offenses punishable by finds include littering, overstocking an area with trees (called excess), and burying or otherwise illegally disposing of trees.

Speaking to this last point, when you're all alone there on the block, and you're getting paid per tree, the temptation to bury trees or throw them into the woods when no one is looking is strong. After all, each bundle that disappears can make you anywhere from 80 cents to $2.50, all in a manner of seconds. But not only is disposing of trees in this fashion illegal—if you're caught, it's a firing offense and could also earn you a hefty fine—it's unethical, and it's no way to make you feel good about yourself. I have no doubt that every tree planter cheats once in a while, but take some pride in yourself. Even though you may suspect the highballers are cheating when they give their tally at the end of the day, at least you'll feel confident knowing that every tree you claim to have planted actually has a chance at capturing carbon one day.

Once all the above has been decided upon, the planting company is paid for the work and then passes on the money due to each planter. Tree planters usually receive their checks a month or so after completing the season. If planters need money during the season, it is available in the form of a small advance. These are issued on days off and are often limited to $100–$200.

Days off are a big temptation to spend a lot of money treating yourself, because you've been deprived of civilization and creature comforts for so long. Do yourself a favor and take as little as possible in the form of advances. You will thank yourself in the long run.

Tree planters also have a bit of a bad reputation in some towns due to planters in past years trashing hotel rooms or otherwise making asses of themselves while in town. In fact, one year when we pulled into a motel late at night, looking forward to a hot shower after driving for several hours after our long planting day, we were turned away once the owner found out we were tree planters. So, don't make an ass out of yourself on the rare days when you make it into town. Not only will you make life better for yourself, you'll be paying it forward to future tree planters, who otherwise might be held liable for your sins.

Calibrate Your Expectations

Rookies should not be too concerned about making of lot of money in the first few days of work or even the first contract. Instead, slow down and focus on quality and technique. Make sure every tree is planted properly. Watch veteran planters, and see how they do it. One thing you'll notice right away is that veterans rarely look like they're moving quickly. That's because they know every move counts in the form of calories burned and time wasted, so they think before they dig. Learn to read the terrain, so you can find soil easily beneath the debris and between the rocks. Trust me, this becomes second nature over time. If you have any questions, don't be afraid to ask your foreman or a veteran planter (although veterans may be loath to share their secrets). Learning how to plant quality trees right from the start will save you a lot of grief over the long haul. There is nothing worse than having to replant trees for free, but it happens.

Due to the strenuous nature of tree planting, companies offer incentives to encourage planters to stay for the entire season. Such incentives include a reduction in daily camp costs or possibly a bonus payment built into the price paid per tree. As mentioned, most people only plant for the spring season, but some die-hards continue for the entire summer, working enough weeks to qualify for employment insurance, so they can spend the winter skiing or, if they're really annoying, snowboarding.

Because tree planting doesn't last all summer long, it's wise to set yourself up with another job that will fill out what remains of June, July, and August. Many a tree planter has set out in hopes of earning enough in May and June to be able to take the rest of the summer off. This dream rarely comes true for rookie planters. Others start out the season all gung-ho, planning to plant during the summer season as well. However, by the end of the spring season, either they decide they've had enough or they have an injury that prevents them from continuing, and if they haven't made plans for another job to fill out the summer, they could find themselves spending the next semester on a straight diet of ramen noodles—and I'm talking Mr. Noodles here, not Ichiban.

All that to say, anyone who goes tree planting is taking a risk. It's not like other jobs, where you can expect to make a certain amount per week. You may go from making $300/day on one contract to making only $100/day on the next. If fate smiles on you, and you end up getting good contracts with easy planting and a good price per tree, you can make a lot of money. As I mentioned above though, I know some people who have lost money tree planting, because they could not make enough to recoup their expenses.

3

HOW TO GET A JOB AS A TREE PLANTER

You're probably familiar with the saying, "It's not what you know but who you know." Sadly, that saying has a lot to do with getting a job as a tree planter.

The tree planting industry is dominated by a few big players, supplemented by a number of smaller companies (see the end of this chapter for a list of some of the bigger tree planting companies in each province and their contact info). In big companies, head office doesn't do the hiring of individual planters. Instead, this task is handled by supervisors (a.k.a. camp managers). Each supervisor oversees anywhere from two to six foremen, who work together with their supervisor to fill out the crew, with each crew consisting of six to twelve planters. In smaller companies, the company owners—who may also function as supervisors and foremen—hire planters directly.

Supervisors and foremen like to hire people they already know to plant for them, because then they feel confident that the people they hire will work hard and earn them a lot of money. In many cases, foremen and supervisors earn a percentage of whatever their crew makes, although some are non-commission. They also do some planting, if they have time. In most companies, veterans comprise about 70 percent of each crew. Although this is true, veterans are always migrating out of the tree planting business, so there is a constant need for fresh meat to fill the boots of departing veterans. Therefore, most foremen hire at least one rookie per season.

In addition, each year the industry sees a number of rookie foremen and supervisors starting out. They try to get as many veterans as possible on their crew, but that is often difficult, because veterans tend to return to plant with the same supervisors and foremen each year. Thus, rookie foremen and supervisors are often forced to hire rookie planters to fill out their crew. Even so, they will still try to hire people they know, but there is a good chance they will consider other applicants who seem like they can handle the job.

Therefore, if you want to get a job as a tree planter, the first thing you should do is network. Do you know anyone who plants or has planted recently? If so, see if that person will arrange an introduction or give you a recommendation. University campuses are a great place to connect with other tree planters. Put up posters, take out ads, post on message boards, talk loudly about your desire to tree plant while in public spaces, whatever it takes.

If your networking efforts fail—or perhaps in addition to networking—go online and submit an application to the tree planting companies who work in the area in which you'd like to plant. This is the equivalent of cold calling, but every company needs a fresh supply of warm bodies, and if you have a pulse, you qualify.

As a last resort, if you are reading this book and tree planting season is nearly upon you, but you still haven't been able to land a job, you might want to risk heading to a place like Prince George, BC, and literally knocking on the door or a tree planting company or hanging out in places where tree planters are bound to show up (an army surplus or camping equipment store is a good bet). Especially during the first two weeks of the season, lots of would-be planters drop out, so this can create some instant hiring opportunities that allow you to circumvent the typical hiring process.

A word of warning though: Don't just sign up with any company. As in any other industry, the bigger the company, usually, the better it is. It will offer better working and living conditions, better food, better vehicles, better training, higher safety standards, wages for camp setup and takedown, timely payments, and best of all, better pay. This is because the bigger companies tend to have long-term contracts with their clients and do a better job of bidding on contracts, which means you make more money.

When Should You Apply?

If you're planning to go tree planting next spring, don't wait until April to submit your application. While some companies are already looking to hire people in December, most hiring happens in January and February. Even so, it's still possible to land a job in March or April. For instance, if a company suddenly lands a big contract right before the season starts, even though they told you they had no openings back in February, they may suddenly become desperate to fill out their roster, so keep your options open.

Special Information for Foreign Workers

Each year, thousands of foreign visitors come to Canada to work, with many of them doing a stint tree planting. Getting a job in Canada as a foreign worker is a bit tricky, but here are some tips that will get you started.

Canada offers two types of work permits for foreign workers. The first type is an employer-specific permit. This permit allows you to work according to the conditions on your permit, which include: the name of the employer you can work for, how long you can work, and the location where you can work (if applicable). To get one, your prospective employer must apply to Employment and Social Development Canada for something called a Labour Market Opinion. This is their way of determining if there's enough demand for workers in a particular occupation and not enough Canadians available to do the job. If you're thinking of going this route, apply early, because it can take anywhere from six to eight months for an answer.

The second option is an open work permit. This allows you to work for any employer in Canada, except for an employer "who is listed as ineligible on the list of employers who have failed to comply with conditions, or who, on a regular basis, offers striptease, erotic dance, escort services or erotic massages." (That quote is taken verbatim from the Government of Canada's website. So, strike "stripper" off your list of fallback plans after tree planting.) The length of this permit varies from six months to two years, depending on your country or territory of origin. According to the Government of Canada's website, "your country or territory of citizenship must have an agreement with Canada that allows you to apply for an IEC work permit, or you may be able to use a Recognized Organization. You must also meet the eligibility requirements for your country or territory of citizenship and the category you're applying for. Make sure you understand all the requirements before you apply." This is a great option, because it allows you to skip the lengthy Labour Market Opinion process, to work for multiple employers, and to work anywhere in the country. So, once you're done planting, you can try something easier, like renting out your body to be used for scientific experiments or working at the customer service counter at Walmart. For more information on how to apply for these permits, visit http://www.cic.gc.ca/english/work/iec/eligibility.asp.

Directory of Tree Planting Companies

The following is a list of some of the largest tree planting companies in Canada. Please note that a company's presence on this list should not be interpreted as an endorsement of that company, but most of them have been around for years, if not decades, so there is a good chance they treat their workers right. Most companies offer a lot of information on their website about what the planting experience is like, what they offer, and how to apply to work for them. Some of them also do jobs other than tree planting, so they may also be a source of post-tree planting work. If you'd like to get the real scuttlebutt on these companies, I recommend going to www.replant.ca, www.hardcoretreeplanters.com, or www.tree-planter.com to find out what other planters have to say about them.

If at any point you feel like you're being mistreated, or your rights are being violated, don't hesitate to contact the Employment Standards complaint service in the province in which you're planting. Apart from that, here are some good questions to ask each company before signing on with them.

- How will I be paid and how often?
- What factors could affect my pay? (e.g. holdbacks, bonuses, equipment costs, camp costs, etc.)

- What are the travel, accommodation, and meal arrangements?
- What is the daily deduction for camp costs?
- What equipment do I have to provide?
- Can I have the names and contact information for two or three people who planted with your company last year?

Alberta

BRINKMAN & ASSOCIATES REFORESTATION LTD.
520 Sharpe St., New Westminster, BC V3M 4R2
Phone: (604) 521-7771
www.brinkmanreforestation.ca

HERITAGE REFORESTATION
1418 Mt. St. Patrice, Dacre, ON K0J 1N0
Phone: 1 (877) 324-4448
www.heritageinc.ca

LEGACY REFORESTATION
Email: legacyreforestation@gmail.com
www.legacyreforestation.ca

OUTLAND
5915 Airport Road, Mississauga, ON L4V 1T1
Email: outland@outland.ca
www.outlandplanting.ca

RHINO REFORESTATION
www.rhinoreforestation.ca

SHAKTI REFORESTATION
310-10654 82nd Ave., Edmonton, AB T6E 2A7
Phone: (780) 328-0958
Email: admin@shaktitrees.com
www.shaktitrees.com

SPECTRUM RESOURCES GROUP
103-11312 98th Ave., Grande Prairie, AB T8V 8H4
Phone: (780) 832-0362
Email: srgi@srgi.ca
www.srgi.ca

British Columbia

AKEHURST & GILTRAP (A+G) REFORESTATION
480 Keith Rd., West Vancouver, BC V7T 1L7
Phone: (778)-344-1837
Email: info@agreforeststation.ca
www.agreforestation.ca

ALL-STARS SILVICULTURE LTD.
207 Larsen Ave., Enderby, BC V0E 1V2
Phone: (250) 308-2785
Email: allstarssilviculture@gmail.com

ARTISAN REFORESTATION
Box 2330, Fort St. James, BC V0J 1P0
Email: peter@artisanreforestation.com
www.artistanreforestation.com

BLUE COLLAR REFORESTATION
255 Lear Road, Quesnel, BC V2J 5V5
Phone: (250) 992-9709
Email: etienne@bluecollargroup.ca
www.bluecollargroup.ca

BRINKMAN AND ASSOCIATES REFORESTATION LTD.
520 Sharpe St., New Westminster, BC V3M 4R2
Phone: (604) 521-7771
www.brinkmanreforestation.ca

CELTIC REFORESTATION SERVICES LTD.
1991 1st Ave., Prince George, BC V2L 2Z1
Phone: (250) 562-2535
Email: admin@celticreforestation.com
www.celticreforestation.com

COAST RANGE CONTRACTING
Email: melissa@coastrange.ca
www.coastrange.ca

DYNAMIC REFORESTATION
Box 4129, Williams Lake, BC V2G 2V2
Phone: (250) 398-9478
Email: info@dynamicreforestation.com
www.dynamicreforestation.com

FOLKLORE CONTRACTING
1077 Eastern Street, Prince George, BC V2N 5R8
Phone: (250) 563-5765
Email: info@folklorecontracting.ca
www.folklorecontracting.ca

HERITAGE REFORESTATION
1418 Mt. St. Patrice, Dacre, ON K0J 1N0
Phone: 1 (877) 324-4448
www.heritageinc.ca

POINTS WEST FORESTRY
Prince George, BC
Email: u2pointswest@hotmail.com
www.facebook.com/pg/pointswestforestry

QUASTUCO SILVICULTURE LTD.
11-477 Martin Street, Penticton, BC V2A 5L2
Phone: (250) 809-8619

Email: Scott.quastuco@shaw.ca
www.quastuco.com

RHINO REFORESTATION
www.rhinoreforestation.ca

SPECTRUM RESOURCES GROUP
3810 18th Ave., Prince George, BC V2N 4V5
Phone: (250) 564-0383
Email: srgi@srgi.ca
www.srgi.ca

SUMMIT REFORESTATION
PO Box 2786, Smithers, BC V0J 2N0
Phone: (250) 847-5125
Email: info@summitreforestation.com
www.summitplanting.com

WINDFIRM RESOURCES INC.
Box 3292, Smithers, BC V0J 2N0
Phone: (250) 847-1405
Email: office@windfirm.ca
www.windfirm.ca

Manitoba

LEGACY REFORESTATION
Email: legacyreforestation@gmail.com
www.legacyreforestation.ca

OUTLAND
5915 Airport Road, Mississauga, ON L4V 1T1
Email: outland@outland.ca
www.outlandplanting.ca

Ontario

BRINKMAN & ASSOCIATES REFORESTATION LTD.
520 Sharpe St., New Westminster, BC V3M 4R2
Phone: (604) 521-7771
www.brinkmanreforestation.ca

HAVEMAN BROTHERS
Box 249, Kakabeka Falls, ON P0T 1W0
Phone: (807) 475-4662
Email: info@havemanbrothers.com
www.havemanbrothers.com

HERITAGE REFORESTATION
1418 Mt. St. Patrice, Dacre, ON K0J 1N0
Phone: 1 (877) 324-4448
www.heritageinc.ca

OUTLAND
5915 Airport Road, Mississauga, ON L4V 1T1
Email: outland@outland.ca
www.outlandplanting.ca

THUNDERHOUSE FOREST SERVICES INC.
Box 70, 37 Rouse St., Hearst, ON P0L 1N0
Phone: (705) 362-4488
mail@thunderhouse.ca
www.thunderhouse.ca

TREELINE REFORESTATION
Box 670 Englehart, ON P0J 1H0
Phone: (705) 544-1142
www.treeline.on.ca

Quebec

OUTLAND
5915 Airport Road, Mississauga, ON L4V 1T1
Email: outland@outland.ca
www.outlandplanting.ca

COOPÉRATIVE FORESTIÈRE DE LA PETITE NATION
761, chemin des Pionniers, La Minerve, QC J0T 1S0
Phone: (819) 274-2442
Email: cfpn@qc.aira.com

COOPÉRATIVE FORESTIÈRE NEW-RICHMOND–ST-ALPHONSE
121, route de Saint-Alphonse, Saint-Alphonse, QC G0C 2V0
Phone: (418) 388-5481
Email: cfna.benoit@globetrotter.net

COOPÉRATIVE FORESTIÈRE DE PETIT PARIS
576, rue Gaudreault, St-Ludger-de-Milot, QC G0W 2B0
Phone: (418) 373-2575
www.cfpp.com

COOPÉRATIVE FORESTIÈRE GIRARDVILLE
2077, rang Saint-Joseph Nord, Girardville, QC G0W 1R0
Phone: (418) 258-3451
Email: snadeau@epicea.org
www.epicea.org

LA FORÊT DE DEMAIN
200, 6ème rue ouest, Amos, QC J9T 2T5
Phone: (819) 727-5556

LA FORESTERIE ASL INC.
803 14ièm avenue, Senneterre, QC J0Y 2M0
Phone: 819-737-8851

Email: cathy.tremblay@foresterieasl.ca
www.foresterieasl.ca

LES REBOISEURS DE LA PÉNINSULE
355 av de Port-Royal, Bonaventure, QC G0C 1E0
Phone: 418-534-3979
Email: vincent_chabot@hotmail.com

Special Bonus Section: New Zealand!

If you've ever dreamed of visiting this beautiful country, why not leave them something to remember you by, like tens of thousands of trees? Seeing as their seasons are the opposite of ours, this is the perfect way to spend your off season, seeing incredible Kiwi vistas while earning some cash! Here's the contact info for one company to get you started.

NATIVE SOLUTIONS
Box 631, Rangiora, North Canterbury 7400, New Zealand
Phone: (03) 312 8399
Email: info@nativesolutions.co.nz
www.nativesolutions.co.nz

4

WHAT IT COSTS TO TREE PLANT AND WHAT YOU'LL NEED TO DO IT

Now that you have a good idea of how much money you can make as a tree planter, it's a good time to look at what you need to get started and how much cash you'll have to plunk down before you get started. Your up-front costs can be divided into three main areas: 1) planting equipment, 2) personal gear, and 3) transportation expenses (to and from the area where you'll be planting). Here's a breakdown of each category.

Transportation

Your transportation costs will be affected by the distance between where you live and where you are going to plant and how you plan to get there. It's quicker to fly, of course, but it's also more expensive. You can drive, but carting your vehicle from site to site can be a bit of a hassle, and it isolates you from the rest of the crew. (Travel time is also bonding time.) The rough logging roads can also do a number on your vehicle and your windshield. Some companies allow you to park your vehicle in town at their worksite. Check with them beforehand to see if this is an option.

Rather than drive on your own, you can also check around to see if anyone else in your area is going planting. Then you can carpool, which will save you money and cut down on CO_2 emissions. I would recommend taking the bus as another option, but Greyhound has ceased service in Western Canada, so that option is no longer on the table. If all else fails, there's always hitchhiking. However, even though I've hitchhiked and picked up hitchhikers from time to time, I don't officially endorse this option.

Tree Planting Gear

Your first step when it comes to planting gear should be to check with your company to see if they will supply you with any equipment. Some companies have a good supply of used or new gear that they sell or rent to planters. Sometimes you have to pay up front, and sometimes the cost of the gear is deducted from your earnings. New and used planting gear is also available in specialized equipment stores in towns that are central to tree planting. Your company can recommend where to buy it. (I've also included a list of stores at the end of this chapter.) Another good source for used gear is Kijiji or Craig's List. As mentioned earlier, veterans are always migrating out of the field, and those who are may be looking to get rid of their gear, so keep your eyes open.

Speaking of which, if you get to the end of your season and decide you've had enough of tree planting to last for the rest of your life, you can often take your gear back to the place where you bought it (if your gear is still in good shape), and they will buy it back from you at a reduced rate. That said, don't be too quick to dump your gear after your first season, even if, at that point, you swear you will never go tree planting again. Time has a way of warming the heart and causing us to forget about the bad times—like that day a hailstorm hit us once, circled around the valley, and came back and hit us again—and remember the good times, like the moment when you looked up suddenly and found yourself face to face with a moose about twenty feet away from you, quietly munching grass as it stared curiously at the grubby, tree-laden, shovel-wielding creature that had invaded its territory.

Okay, so let's get down to the basis of what you're going to need in this department.

- **Shovel:** This is the equivalent of a rifle for a Marine. It's your best friend throughout your planting season, so treat it well. Even name it, if you feel so inclined. Tree planters use one of three types of shovels: regular D-handle shovels, speed shovels, and staff-handle shovels. D-handle shovels are about waist height and have a long narrow blade. Speed shovels also have a D-handle but have a shorter blade and shaft. A staff-handled shovel can have either type of blade, but it has a long handle on it, like a hoe or a rake. This type of shovel is often used by planters who have developed tendonitis in their writs. Most planters—and all rookies—start out with a regular D-handle shovel. Check with your company before you buy. You can always change or upgrade mid-season. Some companies even allow you to customize your shovel before you order it. When buying a used shovel, make sure the shaft is solid, the handle isn't cracked, and that the blade isn't cracked and has no major notches or chips in it.

- **Planting bags:** The bags used for tree planting are made of a heavy rubber material. They cinch around your waist and also have shoulder straps to help ease the burden. Each set includes three bags in total—one on each hip and one in the rear. The hip bags are used to hold bundles of trees. The rear bag can also be used to hold trees, but you may also reserve it for other items, such as snacks, bug spray, and your water bottle.

- **Silvicool bag inserts:** These are bags that you place inside your planting bags to protect your seedlings from the elements. They are made of a white plastic material on the outside and lined with "silvicool" foil, with a drawstring at the top. You will need at least two of these, although I recommend getting a third one to go in your rear bag or in case one of the other bags gets damaged.

- **Silvicool tarp:** The is not the same kind of blue tarp that your dad has out in the garage. These tarps are made of the same material as the bag inserts—plastic on one side, silvicool foil on the other. These are used at your individual cache to keep your trees cool. Your tarp can also double as a place to hide out from rain or hail if it gets too ferocious. Buy a new tarp; the bigger the better. And write your name on it! In fact, this last point goes for all your gear. Name it, or someone else might claim it.

- **Gloves:** Special tree planting gloves, such as Ganka Suregrip work gloves, can be purchased at any tree planting equipment store. These gloves are made of a rubberized cloth and do a great job of protecting your hands from cuts and blisters while still making you dexterous enough to feel each tree. Don't bring a pair of your dad's leather work gloves, because they're too thick and clumsy. Gardening gloves are okay, but don't count on them lasting long. Die-hard macho tree planters will tell you that gloves are for wimps. Don't listen to them—unless you also have something to prove. I stupidly didn't wear gloves during my last season of tree planting and wound up on five days of intravenous antibiotics due to an infection from a seemingly minor cut in my finger. Many tree planters take a fashion tip from the late Michael Jackson and wear only one glove, usually on the hand they use to put the trees into the ground. Other people wrap their fingers in duct tape every day instead of wearing gloves. Some people wear a bicycling glove on their shovel hand and a Ganka glove on their planting hand. To each their own. Just do something to protect your hands.

- **Plot cord:** This is a light cable measuring device (about ten feet long) used to take plots in an area to determine if you have planted the right number of trees to the required level of quality (see the glossary for more details).

- **Water bottle:** I recommend a two-liter bottle at the minimum. Better to bring a full gallon. Dehydration can be a real problem when planting in hot weather. Be careful, because it can sneak up on you and wipe you out—or put you in the hospital. In addition to the big bottle, which you can store at your cache, bring along a smaller bottle that you can carry with you as you plant. You may also want a thermos, so you can have a hot cup of coffee to give you a pick-me-up after lunch.

- **Block bag:** This is a small backpack used to carry extra clothes, rain gear, your lunch, toilet paper, your phone, and other items to and from the block. If you have any electronics with you, it's a good idea to also invest in a waterproof stuff sack.

- **Rain gear:** Rain gear can be expensive, but don't think you can get away without it. Some seasons, it never rains, and some seasons, it never stops raining—or hailing, sleeting, or snowing. During other seasons, it rains only thirty minutes a day—just enough time to get everything good and wet. Whatever the case, tree planters work in all kinds of weather. So, buy quality rain gear—jacket and pants. You will thank yourself when you look out from under your hood and see the guy next to you planting while wearing a green garbage bag. Army surplus stores are a good source of rugged rain gear at a reasonable price, but you can also look at places like Canadian Tire, Mountain Equipment Co-op (MEC), and Cabela's.

- **Gaiters:** Gaiters strap over your boots and around your leg to provide protection from branches and thorns and to prevent mud, snow, and dirt from entering the top of your boots.

- **Boots:** I saved this item for last, because it's the most important. Buying good boots is the best investment a tree planter can make. The ruggedness of tree planting demands tough boots with firm ankle support and something that will help absorb the impact of pounding your foot down on your shovel and while closing a hole hundreds or thousands of times per day. Water resistance is also a must. Oddly enough, the best boots you can buy for tree planting are ice-climbing boots. These are like the old molded plastic hockey skates you may have had as a kid. They have a hinged ankle and a cloth bootie on the inside that can be removed for cleaning and drying purposes. You can count on these boots lasting for your entire planting career, which is good, because they are expensive, costing up to $500. The most popular option are orange caulks. The advantages of these boots is they are waterproof, and the caulks or spikes on the bottom make screefing—clearing away debris—much easier, as does the steel toe. They are also a lot cheaper than the ice-climbing option. The downfall of orange caulks is they tend to be quite hot. Army boots is another option. (I spent two seasons planting in them, though I don't recommend it.) They are quite cheap compared to the other options, waterproof for the first few weeks at least, and will last a season. The major disadvantages to army boots are the cheaper ones don't have a steel toe, and they don't protect your feet enough from the pain of constantly stomping on your shovel. Finally, there's the classic leather work boot. Some brands last, and others don't. Word to the wise: if your boots have laces, bring an extra pair of laces with you.

Personal Gear

My first piece of advice here is to bring a minimal amount of personal gear. Tree planters tend to move around a lot. The less stuff you have, the easier it is to move, and the harder it is to lose. Also, tree planting vehicles have a limited amount of room for gear, and you don't want to be the prima donna pulling up with three roller bags and a lap dog in tow. Here's a list of some must-have items.

- **Luggage:** I advocate housing all your personal gear in a large backpack, hockey bag, or, better yet, a large dry bag that is normally used for canoeing (available at Mountain Equipment Co-op and other stores that sell outdoor gear). This will keep your gear dry when it's tossed into the back of a pick-up truck and it rains on the way to the planting site. No matter which luggage option you choose, whatever doesn't fit stays home. No second bags allowed!

- **Tent:** A free-standing dome tent is your best bet. If you don't already have a tent, I recommend a three-person tent, even if you're the only one using it. That way you'll have plenty of room for your gear, and you won't wind up accidentally brushing against the sides of the tent when it's raining, which is a great way to soak your sleeping bag. In addition, make sure your tent has a full fly. Even better is a fly that extends past the tent to create a waterproof vestibule. Then you don't have to bring your dirty planting gear and stinky clothes inside.

- **Tent pegs:** I don't care what kind of tent pegs your tent comes with—throw them out. Then go down to your local hardware store and buy some eight- to ten-inch spikes. These are invaluable for driving into rocky ground. While you're at it, you may also want to buy a hammer, but a big rock works well too.

- **Tarp:** This *is* the old blue tarp that your dad has out in the garage. This can be used to put over your tent to provide extra protection against rain and to keep your tent cool when it's hot out. It should be about 1.5–2 times the square footage of your tent. Then, if you extend it out over the area in front of your tent, you will have a nice dry spot to leave your boots and dirty clothes overnight. If you want to spend a bit more money, Mountain Equipment Co-op has some excellent lightweight tarps, such as the Silicone Guides' Tarp, that are quick and easy to string up, and they pack down to the size of a pair of wool socks.

- **Ground sheet:** This is a tarp that you put under your tent to prevent moisture from wicking up out of the ground and to prevent you from poking holes in your tend floor. Make sure it is about the same size as your tent floor with not much sticking out around the edges, or else it could just become a water trap.

- **Mattress:** At the very minimum, get a backpacking foamy. A more comfortable option is a self-inflating air mattress—until you poke a hole in it, that is. Little comforts like this make a huge difference when planting.

- **Sleeping bag:** Cold nights and frigid mornings are the rule for most of the spring season. You'll be at elevation, and you may see patches of snow on the ground. If you don't already have a sleeping bag, buy one that's rated for at least five degrees below zero (Celsius!). A mummy bag with synthetic filling is the best option (avoid down, which does not insulate when wet). If you can't afford a new bag, bring an extra blanket and a sheet to put inside. It's amazing what layering up will do. I've also slept in mitts and a toque (beanie) on frigid nights. To keep your sleeping bag clean, I recommend buying a liner as well. And for the love of God, shower before you go to bed!

- **Pillow:** I realize pillows take up room, but like a good mattress, having a good pillow can make all the difference. Don't fool yourself into thinking you can just bring along a pillowcase and stuff it with clothes. I've done it, and it's awful. Bringing an extra pillow case is also a good idea. Even though you shower every night (right?), you'll still probably want to burn your pillow case or throw it away at the end of the season.

- **Clothes:** Bring as few clothes as possible—that goes for planting clothes as well as street clothes for after work and on days off. If you bring more than you need, they'll just clutter up your tent, and you won't wear half of them anyway. Clothes can be washed in town on days off, and some longer-term camps even have laundry facilities on site. Either way, be prepared to go at least five days without doing laundry. I recommend two pairs of planting clothes, something to wear around camp at night after you shower, something to sleep in (long underwear is great on cold nights), and your swimsuit. (Ladies: word has it that sports bras are a life saver while out on the block, so take heed.) Planting clothes should include two to three pairs of rugged pants (army pants are a good choice), several T-shirts, and two long-sleeved shirts or sweaters. Avoid natural fibers, such as cotton. Stick to synthetics instead. They dry quicker and keep you cooler (or warmer, as the case may be). You may also find an old jacket useful. When planting, think like a hiker and dress in layers, because the weather can change considerably throughout the day. It's actually good to feel a bit cold starting out, because you'll warm up quickly. Something you don't want to scrimp on are underwear and socks. I recommend putting on a fresh pair every day. You'll feel better, and you'll smell better. You may also want to purchase Barna socks, little booties that go over your socks. These are especially helpful if you're planting in rubber boots, because they cut down on friction. Finally, be prepared to throw away all your planting clothes at the end of the season. They'll almost certainly be stained, torn, and otherwise destroyed.

- **Rope:** This is great for clotheslines, tying up your tarp, holding up your pants, it's good for everything! In fact, one time we used a quad to pull a half-ton truck out of the mud using nothing more than quarter-inch poly rope looped a dozen times between the quad and the truck's bumper. You can buy cheap yellow poly, but climbing rope is another reasonably priced option.

- **Duct tape:** This is the tree planter's best friend and another all-around useful item. You can fix practically anything with duct tape, including your shovel, your rain gear, and even your car!

- **Lunch kit:** I recommend a plastic container (or containers) with a lid that you can use to take your lunch to the block each day.

- **Swiss army knife:** These can be used for everything from opening tree boxes to opening beer bottles. They're also handy for peeling the stickers off boxes, which you'll need to do to keep track of how many boxes of trees you plant in a day. Get a good knife, and it will last you for the rest of your life. A Leatherman is another option.

- **Bug repellant:** This is a must. The best kind to buy is something like Muskol or another type of repellent that has a high level of DEET in it. All those chemicals probably aren't good for your skin, but neither are hundreds of black fly bites. One bottle should last you the season, depending on how much you use, but you can always restock on your day off. An additional item that you might find handy is a mosquito net, a wire and mesh hat that hangs down to cover your face and neck. It looks like a miniature bee-keeper's hat. They can be hot and make it difficult to see, but they can also bring you some much-needed relief from the incessant bugs. While we're at it, mosquito coils may also provide you some relief when back at camp.

- **Lip balm:** I never use lip balm in my daily life, but when it comes to tree planting, this is a must. One year I realized I had developed a habit of licking my lips with every tree I planted. That habit, combined with the heat and the dust and exhaustion, caused me to get the worst cold sores I have ever had. Get a high-quality lip balm, preferably one with sunscreen.

- **Sunscreen:** You're going to be outside all day every day, so make sure you protect your skin from sun damage with a high-SPF sunscreen. Don't count on the dirt and dust to do the trick.

- **Hat:** I recommend a hat for the same reason I recommend sunscreen. Ideally, choose a wide-brimmed hat. You can find a good selection at a place like MEC (Mountain Equipment Co-op). You'll look ridiculous, but not only will it protect you from the sun, it will also reduce the square footage of skin available to the black flies and mosquitoes. Many companies now require you to wear a hard hat when planting, so check with your company beforehand.

- **Wristwatch:** I realize you'll have your phone with you, but your battery may die, or it may get squashed or soaked, and then you'll have no idea what time it is. Knowing the time when planting is critical, because it helps you ensure you're on pace for the day and planting your target number of trees per hour. Leave your Rolex at home though, and buy a cheap watch at Walmart before you go.

- **Towel and facecloth:** Bring along two of each. I recommend dark colors, because as much as you try to keep them clean, they're going to get stained and dirty.

- **First-aid supplies:** All camps will have qualified first-aid responders on staff, but it never hurts to have some of your own first-aid equipment—in fact, it hurts if you don't! Some key items to include are hydrogen peroxide and/or Polysporin to prevent or treat infections, band-aids, moleskin (great for preventing or protecting blisters), Tylenol or Advil, tweezers to pull out the inevitable slivers, and a tensor bandage.

- **Medications:** If you are on any type of medications or have allergies, ensure you bring along an adequate supply. Even if you don't typically have allergies, bring some antihistamines along just in case.

- **Foot powder:** If your feet are sweating in your boots all day, you're liable to get "pickle foot," which is kind of what happens if you stay in a hot tub for too long. The problem is, all that moisture weakens the skin on your feet, making them liable to blisters. So, some foot powder, such as Gold Bond Medicated Powder, can be life saver. Incidentally, Gold Bond is great for other areas of your body too. I'll leave it to you to figure out what those are.

- **Flashlight/headlamp:** Once again, I realize your phone has a light on it, but it never hurts to have another small flashlight or headlamp to read with in your tent at night or to go to and from the toilet. Another option is a gas-powered Coleman lantern, which will also help heat your tent. Keep in mind that it's not good to use such an item in an enclosed space for long. Battery-powered lanterns are also available. These are nice, because you can hang them from the roof of your tent or set them on the ground rather than have to hold them.

- **Bear spray:** Bears are a constant presence and annoyance around camp (see the health and safety chapter for more details). Dangerous bear encounters are rare, but it's wise to keep a can of bear spray on you at all times just in case.

- **Whistle:** I don't want to scare anyone, but this is another good item to have on hand in case of a negative wildlife encounter or an accident or injury. Often you may be planting out of sight of others, so blowing your whistle is a good way to alert people that you're in distress.

- **Plastic bags:** Here I'm talking about garbage bags, grocery bags, and Ziploc bags. It's good to keep a ready supply on hand to help keep your gear organized, keep your clean clothes separate from your dirty clothes, to use as garbage bags, to keep your toilet paper and cellphone dry, and so on.

- **Reading material:** Reading before you go to bed is a great way to unwind from a long day on the block. Books and magazines are one option. Another great option is Kindle or Kobo, because then you don't have to pack anything with you but your phone or your e-reader.

- **Back-up battery:** This is handy in case your phone runs out of juice.

Charge it each night (your camp will have generators running), and you'll have plenty of power throughout the day.

- **Pen and paper:** You never know when inspiration will strike. Use it to journal about your season or to write down that million-dollar idea that occurred to you one day while out on the block. Another item in this category is a permanent marker, which you can use to label your gear.

- **Playing cards:** Card games are another great way to unwind and socialize after a long day of work. And if you can't find anyone else who wants to play, there's always solitaire.

- **Toilet paper:** The camp will supply it, but I keep an extra roll on hand while you're planting in case of emergency. And if you're foolish enough to refill your water bottle out of a nearby stream, you will have emergencies. Stick the roll in a waterproof bag, so it stays dry. There are substitutes while out on the block, such as leaves, moss, or ripping off the sleeve of your T-shirt, but if you're like me, you like the real thing, the softer the better. And if someone else on the block forgets a roll, a square of toilet paper can be as valuable as a cigarette in prison, so bargain wisely!

- **Baby wipes:** Don't laugh at this. Even special forces soldiers bring baby wipes with them on patrol. A small pack is a handy item to clean up if a good water source isn't available.

- **Hand sanitizer:** It doesn't hurt to have some of this along, especially if you want to clean your hands out on the block prior to eating. It won't get rid of the pesticide and herbicide residue from the seedlings, but it'll at least kill the germs.

- **Toiletries:** Bring plenty of toothpaste, an extra toothbrush, shaving gear, DEODORANT, soap, shampoo, hand lotion, feminine hygiene products, and everything else you need to keep yourself clean, healthy, and odor-free throughout the season.

- **Lawn chair:** I admit this is somewhat of a luxury, but there's nothing like being able to sit down in a chair outside your tent and pull off your boots after a long hard day. Lawn chairs are also handy for sitting round the campfire at night. Another option is a folding camp stool.

- **Podcasts:** This isn't something you pack, but I thought I should mention it here anyway. While you're in town or in range of Wi-Fi source (some camps provide Wi-Fi), download as many episodes of your favorite podcasts as your phone will hold. The same goes for music and TV shows. This is a great way to help you endure the monotony of planting tree after tree after tree after tree . . . .

The Bottom Line

How much is all this gear going to cost? That all depends on how much of this gear you already own, how much gear you plan to bring, the quality of gear you purchase, and whether you buy used or new. Overall, count on spending at least $500 and as much as $1,000 or even $1,500 if you go for a high-end tent, boots, and so on. It's a lot of money, and it's a bit of a risk, seeing as you don't even know if you'll survive the season, but most of the gear is good to have on hand anyway. And as I said, if things don't work out, you should be able to recoup some of the money you spend on planting gear by re-selling it.

Where to Buy Your Gear

As mentioned, your employer will be able to give you some direction on this, but here are some great places to start. Suppliers marked with a * specialize in planting gear as well as other outdoor gear.

- **Bushpro*** (www.bushpro.ca)
- **Cabela's** (www.cabelas.ca)
- **Canadian Tire** (www.canadiantire.ca)
- **The Forestry Store*** (https://theforestrystore.com)
- **Gear Up for Outdoors*** (www.gear-up.com)
- **Mountain Equipment Co-op** (www.mec.ca)
- **Workwizer*** (www.workwizer.ca)

5

HEALTH AND SAFETY

As should be clear by now, tree planting is one of the most strenuous jobs you can do. Not only do you expend thousands of calories each day, you're exposed to the elements constantly, including the sun, rain, wind, hail, sleet, snow, lightning, black flies, mosquitoes, wasps, bees, wild animals, tainted stream water, cold, heat, and pretty much anything else Nature can throw your way. As a result, it's natural for your body to get run down, which makes you more susceptible to sickness.

In addition, the repetitive nature of the work can create all sorts of other problems, including tendonitis in your shovel hand, heel spurs, lower-back pain, blisters, cuts, abrasions, and chafing. For example, if you have hairy legs, like I do, pay attention to your outer thighs, which your tree planting bags rub against constantly, and watch as the hair in those spots disappears. (Don't worry, it'll grow back!)

General Tips

To help you prevent and/or treat some of the injuries you may suffer as a tree planter, here are some pointers.

- **Bathe regularly:** It may seem strange to have to tell you this, but after a long, hard day on the block, especially during your first week or two as your body is becoming accustomed to the job, you might be tempted to skip the shower and go straight to bed. Don't do it. Not only will taking a shower make you feel and smell better, it will also reduce your chances of developing uncomfortable and unsightly skin conditions, such as rashes and infections.

- **Get plenty of sleep:** The surest way to get sick is to let yourself get worn down by staying up late partying or doing other foolish things. You're going to work hard, so sleep hard. You can party when the season's over.

- **Eat well:** Most camps have excellent cooks, and food is never in short supply. So, if you love food, you'll be in pig heaven. You'll be paying anywhere from $15–$35 a day for camp fees, which includes your food, so make the most of it! And if you're worried about gaining weight, remember, you're going to be burning calories like a marathon runner, so dig in! And by the way, before you eat, wash your hands! This includes when you're out on the block. The seedlings could have chemical or residue on them from fertilizers or pesticides and herbicides, and you may have used your hands to apply bug repellant, so, at the very least, rinse your hands using your water bottle.

- **Hydrate:** Dehydration can sneak up on you if you're not careful, so don't hold back on the water, especially if it's hot out. Even in cooler weather, you're going to be sweating constantly, and the wind is constantly wicking moisture away from your body without you realizing it. Even so, no matter how thirsty you are, DO NOT drink from any natural water sources. When I was young, I was told that if stream is running over rocks for a long stretch, the water is probably safe to drink, because it naturally filters itself. That may or may not be true. However, even the cleanest and purest looking water can be infected with bacteria due to a dead animal upstream, animal feces, and the like. Your camp will supply you with plenty of fresh, clean water, so no matter how good it looks, don't drink the natural stuff. Beaver fever is no treat. And if you don't know what that is, look it up.

- **Don't ignore injuries:** I'm speaking to myself here. Even a minor cut or scrape can quickly become infected while tree planting. I ignored just such a scrape on my finger, which is what landed me in the hospital on intravenous antibiotics. There's no way to avoid the dirt out there, so if you get cut, hit the disinfectant hard, bandage it up, and keep an eye on it. The same goes for blisters. Disinfect them, bandage them, and then slap some moleskin over top to protect the area. And change your dressing daily, so you can do a visual check to ensure infection hasn't set in. If you notice anything strange, go to the camp's first-aid personnel to get it checked out. You don't want to waste time driving into town, which could be hours away, because you were too lazy to deal with things properly in the first place. It could cost you hundreds of dollars in lost revenue.

In addition to cuts, abrasions, and blisters, another common affliction is tendonitis. This is caused by repetitive motion that eventually strains the muscles and tendons around a joint. The most common place to get it is in the wrist of the hand you use to jam your shovel into the ground, particularly if you're planting in rocky terrain. You will know you're getting tendonitis if your wrist starts to hurt and you hear or feel a grinding in your wrist. Sometimes a wrist brace or tensor bandage can alleviate the condition. Using a staff-handle shovel for a while also helps, because it changes the motion. If neither of these help, and you feel the condition is getting worse instead of better, it may be time to consider whether you need to pack up your bags and go home—but not before filing a claim with Workers' Compensation.

Speaking of which, safety is a top priority in every workplace, including out in the wilderness. If you witness any unsafe activities, such as unsafe driving, or if you feel you're being asked to do a task that could endanger you in any way, speak to your foreman or supervisor about it. If they don't listen, don't hesitate to contact the Employment Standards Branch. Their contact information is available online.

Physical Preparation for Tree Planting

Preparing yourself physically to go tree planting won't guarantee you'll have a successful season, but it can reduce the risk of injury, soreness, and fatigue and also increase your earning potential. But no matter how much physical preparation you do, almost nothing matches the rigors of tree planting, so be prepared for some sore muscles, especially during the first couple of weeks.

Some good pre-planting exercises include activities that build your cardio capacity, such as hiking and walking, preferably wearing a backpack with some weight in it. Cross-country skiing, snowshoeing, and running are also effective. Tree planting taxes your legs, so do some exercises to help build them up. Examples include cycling, lunges, squats, and burpees. Body-weight and core exercises, such as push-ups and sit-ups are also helpful. Whatever you do, remember that the goal is endurance, not speed and power. Train like a marathon runner or a triathlete rather than a bodybuilder. Big muscles might look great in the mirror, but they aren't much good out on the block.

And don't wait until a week before tree planting season to get started. Ideally, you should train for a least a couple of months beforehand to ensure you're in tip-top shape.

A Word About Wildlife

While planting, I've had close encounters with moose, elk, deer, eagles, enormous toads, black bears, and grizzlies. It's pretty cool—one of the perks of tree planting—but Nature is not a zoo. As Charles Darwin said, it's red in tooth and claw. So, no matter how cute and cuddly the critter looks or how docile it seems, give it plenty of space.

This is a good place to bring up bears. You can count on you or someone else on your crew encountering a bear or bears during your tree planting season. I've watched them steal lunches from planters' caches, found bear footprints on the tables in our mess tent one morning, and one year, we woke up to find a big black bear sleeping on top of our van.

If you do encounter a bear, the first rule is, don't panic. Most often, even big, ferocious-looking creatures like grizzlies want nothing to do with you. Their goal is to get as far away from you as quickly as possible. So, don't run away, or you may actually trigger the sort of aggressive behavior you were trying to avoid. Stand your ground, make some noise (use your whistle), and make yourself look as big as possible. Then slowly back away, keeping your eyes on the bear and one hand on your handy dandy can of bear spray. (You did bring bear spray, right?)

If you have any food on you, you might be tempted to throw it to the bear as a distraction. Don't do it. This just teaches bears that humans are a source of food. It may save your skin, but it may cause the bear to be aggressive with the next human it meets, especially if that person doesn't also cough up some free lunch.

If a bear decides to get aggressive, while blowing your whistle or yelling, pull out your pepper spray, and shoot a couple of warning shots. Make sure you're not downwind from it though, or you might get the brunt of it. In most cases, that will be enough to send the bear packing.

If the bear continues to approach, continue shooting pepper spray at it. You may even want to drop your planting bags, which the bear may pause to sniff through, especially if you've packed some snacks, buying you time to get away. If there's a climbable tree nearby, that may offer a handy escape. But remember: black bears are expert tree climbers. I treed a black bear once, and I was amazed to see it shoot up a sixty-five-foot pine tree in about four seconds flat. If all else fails, hit the ground, and play dead. Lie face down with your hands clasped on the back of your neck. This protects your face and vital organs, and it makes it difficult for the bear to flip you over. You might get stomped on, bitten, and knocked around or even buried (sometimes bears do that), but it could just save your life.

One of the key bear attractants is garbage, especially food waste. So, make sure you don't leave any garbage around your tent or where you're planting. A girl on our crew learned this firsthand when she stayed back in camp one day, because she was feeling sick. To help settle her stomach, she ate a banana and then threw the peel out her tent door, intending to put it in the garbage after she had a nap. Instead, she woke up to find a huge black bear squatting outside her tent and peering in at her through the screen door as he munched on the unexpected treat. Thankfully, after a few minutes, it got up and walked away.

My saddest bear encounter wound up with two bears shot dead. I'm not sure what happened, but we woke up one morning to the sound of gunshots. The guy in charge of "protecting" us from bears had killed two sows. He claimed they were a threat, so he had to shoot them. I was pretty upset about that, because I suspect the guy simply had an itchy trigger finger. But the fact was, the bears had been pestering the camp, constantly tearing things apart in search of food. The sad truth is, once a bear becomes habituated to humans and sees them as a source of food, apart from relocation, euthanizing them is often the only option. So do yourself and the bears a favor, and pick up your trash!

CONCLUSION

There you have it! (Almost) everything you need to know about tree planting, all here in this handy-dandy little book. I hope you feel a lot more confident than when you started now that you know what tree planting is, where it happens, how much money you can make, how to get a job doing it, and how to survive the season.

I'm not going to lie to you and say tree planting is the best job ever, because it's not. But if you're looking for adventure, friendship, bragging rights, the opportunity to achieve a level of physical fitness that you never thought possible, and a chance to spend the summer in the great outdoors doing something that literally saves the planet (all while getting paid good money to do it), then tree planting might be the job for you. However, if reading this book already has you quaking in your Birkenstocks, perhaps it's time to look for a less-formidable challenge, like telemarketing. (I've made good money doing that too!)

If you've found this book helpful, I'd love to hear from you. And if you have any comments, criticisms, recommended companies, bad experiences with a particular company, songs, poems, bear stories, new slang terms, I'd like to hear those too—the good, the bad, and the ugly—including photos. Send it all to www.kevinmillerxi.com.

CONCLUSION

GLOSSARY OF TREE PLANTING TERMS

So far you've learned what tree planting is, how to live like a tree planter, how to dress like a tree planter, and even how to think like a tree planter. Now it's time to learn how to talk like a tree planter, so you won't sound like a total doofus on your first day out.

Bare-root seedlings: A type of seedling that does not have its roots encased in a neat little plug of dirt. Instead, it looks more like a bad case of bed head. At first, most planters are intimidated by bare-root seedlings and prefer planting plugs. After some time though, bare-root seedlings tend to grow on a person, so to speak, especially if he or she doesn't shower.

Block: The working term for what the rest of the world knows as a clearcut. It is an area of forest that has had all or nearly all of the trees in it cut down. This is where you'll be planting.

Caulks: Pronounced "corks," these confusing little items are spikes similar to the ones attached to the soles of baseball cleats, which can be screwed into the bottom of your boots to make screefing easier. They also reduce the chance of slipping on a wet log as you attempt to clear a slash pile. This term can also be used to refer to the boots themselves.

Checker: The person employed by the company that issues the contract to ensure all trees are planted to the proper specifications. Supervisors will often throw plots (see below) prior to the checker's arrival to make sure everything is up to snuff.

Cream: This is the kind of land that tree planters dream of and women swoon over. Otherwise known as a "beach," cream land is ground that is free from obstructions, such as duff, rocks, water, stumps, and debris, thus making it easy to plant large numbers of trees in a short period of time. High-probability cream areas include roadsides, mounds, fireguards, and areas that have been hedgerowed, burned, or trenched.

Creamer: You know him or her by other names: opportunist, cherry-picker, or suck-up. This is the weaselly guy or girl who never runs or passes but who stands under the net in a basketball game and expects everyone to pass the ball, so he or she can score. A creamer tries to get all the best land possible by any means necessary. Typical creamer behaviors include "accidentally" cutting in to your section and planting that cream land that you were saving for the last day, finishing early and then planting the cream land nearby before asking the foreman for permission, and generally sucking up to the foreman. Creamers may make a lot of money, but everybody hates them, so don't be one.

Culls: Seedlings that are damaged in some way that makes them unplantable. Some tree planters have elevated the "cultivation" of culls to an art form, seeing as they get paid for the damaged trees. I knew one guy who could cull an entire bundle at once. Of course, if you get caught doing that, you'll be in a lot of trouble.

Duff: Also known as "humus," this is a layer of moss and organic matter that covers the ground. The thickness of the duff layer can vary from an inch or two to over a foot. Most contracts require at least some of the duff to be removed before a seedling is planted. This can be done with your foot or with your shovel, depending on how much duff there is. A good method to measure the area around a seedling that should be duff-free is to use the "hang loose" gesture (pinky and thumb extended out from your fist). How much duff is allowed varies from contract to contract.

Foreman: The person who manages a crew of tree planters. Usually, a crew is composed of six to twelve planters.

Highballer: This is the name for the fastest planter on a crew. Highballers are usually veteran planters. They are fast, because they are skilled at finding the best place to plant their trees in the least amount of time to the specifications of the contract. They are also fast, because they rarely take breaks, and they have learned to cream out fellow planters without getting caught. Many rookies and other non-highballers suspect that Highballers are also adept at planting trees in such unorthodox places as the bottom of cliffs, inside hollow logs, under slash piles, and under water, but that's probably just jealousy speaking.

Landing: A squarish, flattened area on a block that was used by loggers to load trees onto trucks. This area is usually unplantable, because it's so hard packed. Tree planters often use landings as a starting point when planting their sections of the block.

Mounds: A form of scarification used in swampy areas. Mounds are made by a backhoe, forming small piles of dirt. The point of mounds is to create a place where the trees can thrive above the water level.

Naturals: These are the natural offspring of spruce, pine, or fir trees, which can be found intermittently throughout the block. Some contracts require planters to space around naturals as if they were seedlings that the planter has put in the ground. Spotting naturals gets increasingly difficult as the season goes on, because there are a lot of green things growing on clear-cuts.

Plot: A method used by planters and checkers to determine whether or not the trees are being planted according to the specifications of the contract in terms of spacing, depth, root straightness, and screef size. "Throwing a plot" consists of arbitrarily choosing a spot in the planted area (usually by tossing your shovel end over end), sticking your shovel in the ground, looping the plot cord over the shovel, and walking in a circle around the shovel with the plot cord extended to its full length. As you walk in a circle, you count the trees to see if the specified number of trees that should be found in the plot is met, check the spacing (usually about a meter between each tree), and ensure the trees are planted properly. This may involve digging up one or more trees for a closer look.

Plug: A type of seedling whose roots are neatly trimmed and packaged in a cone of dirt. Plugs are the easiest type of seedlings to plant. The cone on a plug may vary from two to seven inches in length.

Reefer: A refrigerated semi-trailer where seedlings are stored when transported from the tree nursery to the block.

Scarification: This refers to anything done to the block to prepare it for reforestation. Scarification has two purposes. First, to ensure the highest possibility of survival for the new seedlings. Second, to make the area easier to plant. At least someone is looking out for tree planters! There are five basic methods of scarification: barrel and chain, burning, mounds, trenching, and windrows.

Screef: This term can be used as a noun and a verb. To screef (v.) is to clear away duff or humus from the area where a seedling is to be planted. A screef (n.) is the area around a tree that has been cleared of debris.

Supervisor: The person in charge of overseeing the foremen for a tree planting company. In a bigger company, a supervisor will typically oversee two to four foremen.

Windrows: These are slash piles that have been bulldozed into rows, making them easier to burn and making it easier to plant.

OTHER TREE PLANTING RESOURCES

While this book provides a good overview of tree planting, if you'd like to take things further, here are a few resources that can help.

Books

- *Eating Dirt: Deep Forests, Big Timber, and Life with the Tree-Planting Tribe* by Charlotte Gill: Winner of the BC National Award for Canadian Non-fiction, this is a memoir of Gill's tree-planting career, which will give you some good insights into the nitty gritty of the tree-planting life.
- *From Our Footsteps, Giant Forests Grow: A Photographic Introspection of British Columbia's Coastal Tree Planting Industry* by Jonathan Clark: While no mere picture can truly capture what tree planting is like, perhaps a collection of photos can. From the author of *Step By Step: A Tree Planter's Handbook* (see below).
- *Pounders* by Josh Barkey: This is a novel about tree planting. A great thing to read before you go or right before bed during your first week on the block.
- *Rite Of Passage: A Photographic Introspective of the Canadian Tree Planting Industry* by Jonathan Clark: More photos of planting life by the man otherwise known as "Scooter."
- *Step By Step, A Tree Planter's Handbook: A Comprehensive Training Guide and Reference Manual* by Jonathan "Scooter" Clark: Clocking in at nearly 500 pages, this book truly *is* a comprehensive guide to tree planting, including everything from detailed instructions on how to plant a tree to how to behave in camp.

While this book focuses mainly on planting in BC, it also includes some information about planting in other provinces and other forestry-related jobs. It's pricey, but if you really want to dig deep into this topic, it's worth the money.

Websites

- **www.hardcoretreeplanters.com:** This site offers a list of tree planting companies, company ratings (you have to sign up to see these, which is free), and best of all, detailed instructions on how to plant a tree. In addition to determination and endurance, technique is everything when it comes to speed as a planter, so this site serves as a good primer prior to getting out in the field.

- **www.tree-planter.com:** This is a comprehensive website that offers up pretty much everything you need to know about tree planting, including links to places where you can purchase tree planting gear.

- **www.replant.ca:** This is another tremendous resource for tree planting information. One of the best aspects of this site is its forum, where you can interact with planters and get a good feel for the latest news and information by scrolling through the various discussion topics.

TREE PLANTING LOG BOOK

Use this tool to keep a record of your progress throughout the season. It's a great way to see how you grow and progress as a tree planter—or not!

DATE	TREES PLANTED	HOURS WORKED	TYPE OF TREE

DATE	TREES PLANTED	HOURS WORKED	TYPE OF TREE

ABOUT THE AUTHOR

Kevin Miller is a prolific author, filmmaker, and former tree planter. He started his planting career in northern BC with TAWA before moving on to Folklore and then returning to his native Saskatchewan to plant in the northern climes of that province (yes, LOTS of trees grow in Saskatchewan!). Kevin now makes his home in Kimberley, BC, and he shudders each morning in the early spring when he sees the tree planters drive by his house on their way to work, but not without a hint of nostalgia about days gone by out on the block. To learn more about Kevin (he writes children's novels and comic books too!), visit www.kevinmillerxi.com.

ENJOYED THIS BOOK?

Then please review it on Amazon.com, Amazon.ca, Goodreads, and anywhere else you can think of. And please recommend it to anyone you know who is thinking about picking up a shovel and pounding thousands of trees into the ground this summer.

www.ingramcontent.com/pod-product-compliance
Lightning Source LLC
Chambersburg PA
CBHW072207170526
45158CB00004BB/1789